30 WAYS
A WIFE CAN BLESS
HER HUSBAND

JOHN TRENT, PH.D.

AspirePress

Torrance, California

AspirePress

30 Ways a Wife Can Bless Her Husband
Copyright © 2015 John Trent
All rights reserved.
Aspire Press, an imprint of Rose Publishing, Inc.
4733 Torrance Blvd., #259
Torrance, California 90503 USA
www.aspirepress.com
Register your book at www.aspirepress.com/register

*Special thanks to Kari Trent and Tamara Love
for their assistance in making these books possible.*

The views and opinions expressed in this book are those of the author(s) and do not necessarily express the views of Aspire Press, nor is this book intended to be a substitute for mental health treatment or professional counseling.

All scripture quotations, unless otherwise indicated, are taken from the New American Standard Bible®, Copyright © 1960, 1962, 1963, 1968, 1971, 1972, 1973, 1975, 1977, 1995 by The Lockman Foundation Used by permission.

Scripture quotations marked (NIV) taken from the Holy Bible, New International Version®, NIV®. Copyright ©1973, 1978, 1984, 2011 by Biblica, Inc.™ Used by permission of Zondervan. All rights reserved worldwide. www.zondervan.com The "NIV" and "New International Version" are trademarks registered in the United States Patent and Trademark Office by Biblica, Inc.™

Scripture quotations marked (ESV) taken from The Holy Bible, English Standard Version Copyright © 2001 by Crossway Bibles, a publishing ministry of Good News Publishers.

Printed in the United States of America
010715RRD

CONTENTS

THE POWER OF A WIFE'S BLESSING

WHEN MY WIFE, Cindy, and I were first married 35 years ago, banking (like so many other things) was done very differently. Today, you can take a picture of a check and transfer funds online, but when we were first married, there was no Internet or even interstate banking! Meaning, when we came home from our honeymoon and got ready to move from Phoenix to Dallas, Cindy actually had to go to her bank and withdraw the six years of teacher retirement funds she'd been carefully saving before we were married.

The problem was she gave that check to me.

We moved to Texas two days after our honeymoon in order for me to start my first job out of graduate school. I had the task of figuring out where we'd bank and what we should do with Cindy's retirement funds that needed to be re-invested.

The bank part was easy. There were tons of banks in Dallas. But I wanted to find just the right place for Cindy's retirement funds to go. That's when I met a person at our church who was an "investment expert."

Problem solved!

Sure, this person had only been an "investment expert" for six months—but he'd worked for the government before that for 25 years. How trustworthy could you get if you'd worked for the federal government! Or at least that's what I thought. This person shared with me an incredible opportunity to invest Cindy's funds into a can't-miss "limited gas and oil partnership." I could *triple* Cindy's retirement funds in no time!

Triple her savings? I couldn't hand over the check fast enough! I also couldn't wait to let Cindy know what a great job I'd done of checking that task off the list. Of course, Cindy asked me if I had really checked into this person's company and background (which I hadn't), and if such a promise was really as good as it sounded.

Being the person I was at the time, her even questioning me angered me. I assured her that her concerns were unfounded. Lots of people had invested with these people. We were lucky to be one of them. And I told her that all she had to do was wait for the oil to gush through the wells we'd invested in—and for her funds to triple . . .

> **I LOST SIX YEARS OF HER TEACHER RETIREMENT FUNDS IN LESS THAN A MONTH.**

Only that's not what happened.

In short, I lost six years of her teacher retirement funds in less than a month. Her savings of six long years evaporated along with my new "advisor" and his company. It was all right there in the Dallas Morning News that morning as I read my paper and choked on my coffee. Which is how I found out that I'd joined a long list of people—most of them people of faith—who had fallen for the "triple-your-money" pitch.

So that night I dragged myself home from work, had Cindy sit down, and handed her the paper. I asked her to read the article—and told her I was sorry and asked her forgiveness for being so blind and dumb.

> BY HER WORDS AND ACTIONS SHE CALLED ME TO BE WHO I COULD BE IN THE FUTURE.

And that's when Cindy had a choice.

I was already totally humiliated. I could have played handball at the curb, I was so low. How could I have been so stupid to have fallen for such a ploy that was so obvious now that my greed had dissolved in light of reality? And me a new PhD!

I deserved for Cindy to pile into me with the "How could you?" words. I figured the couch would be home for several days (or weeks) to come.

What I didn't deserve was what Cindy did that day.

My wife of four months sat at the kitchen table and read the paper. For a long time she didn't say a word. Then she walked over and hugged me for a long time. When she did speak, she told me I was smart and a good husband and that I wasn't the only one who got suckered by the now non-existent firm. She said we'd pray for wisdom together so that something like that never happened again.

And then she said that if she had it to do all over again, she'd still have handed me the check to invest for her.

I can't even begin to tell you how her words just melted my heart—and knitted it to hers. She chose to bless me! She chose to love me—even praise me— when I'd so obviously fallen short. By her words and actions she called me to be who I could be in the future—who we could be together. She "crowned" me with words and actions of blessing.

As I look back on 35 years of marriage, I realize that was just the first time my wife's choice to bless me made an incredible difference in my life.

The Value of Little Choices

There are lots of choices we make each day that really aren't that significant. Turkey sandwich or ham. Soup or salad. Try to get around traffic or sit it out in the lane we're in and tough it out. Catch up on the latest social media posts or head to bed and get some extra sleep. Those choices have minimal impact on our life today or our future tomorrow.

But there are choices that can make a real difference in our life today and tomorrow: Like choosing to be a person who looks to God's Word to be the moral compass of my life, instead of just making decisions based on feelings, trends, or even what our well-intentioned friends think. Like choosing to follow Jesus each day. Like choosing, with God's help and Spirit, to better reflect Jesus to others each and every day. Like choosing to perform small actions that can be an incredibly powerful tool for adding love and life to your marriage as a whole and to your husband's life and future in particular.

Those are the kinds of choices we make each day that really *can* make a *real* difference in who we are today and the person we'll be tomorrow. As C. S. Lewis, a great scholar and Christian, wrote in his book *Mere Christianity*: "Remember, we Christians think man lives forever. Therefore, what really matters is those little marks or twists on the central, inside part of the soul, which are going to turn it, in the long run, into a healthy or hellish creature."

It is indeed those little things we choose to do

in our spiritual and personal life—*including the way we treat our husband at home when no one but our God and our children are watching*—that will set our course for future actions and a healthy relationship.

> **SMALL ACTIONS CAN BE A POWERFUL TOOL FOR ADDING LOVE AND LIFE TO YOUR MARRIAGE.**

Those small choices—which is what this book is all about—are bound up in what C. S. Lewis called "one of the great secrets":

When you are behaving as if you loved someone, you will presently come to love him. . . . Good and evil both increase at compound interest. That is why the little decisions you and I make every day are of such infinite importance. The smallest good act today is the capture of a strategic point from which, a few months later, you may be able to go on to victories you never dreamed of. An apparently trivial indulgence in lust or anger today is the loss of a ridge or railway line or bridgehead from which the enemy may launch an attack otherwise impossible.

The incredible power of little choices is absolutely true for both our faith and our life. And guess where our faith gets lived out first and last.

It's in our home that we live out our faith and where those small choices add up to shape our soul— and our marriage. That just makes sense. Most of us don't start our day at church (unless we live in a parsonage). We may regularly go to church. But it is in our home, where we have the most important earthly relationships, that the rubber meets the road. That's where you and I will make choices and live out the corresponding actions of those choices. Where we will either move closer to our spouse or further away. Where we will choose to have a good attitude or a poor one. Where we will choose to move towards God's best or away from it.

THE BLESSING IS SOMETHING THAT CAN BE GIVEN AND EXPERIENCED IN SMALL WAYS EVERY DAY.

Choosing the Right Path

If you want happiness in your marriage, there *is* a way, a road, a path to travel to achieve a better marriage. There is a path that your family can walk that will lead you towards fulfillment, love, and peace. You really can find the happiness that is offered to each of us, even in our broken world. Even if the family you grew up in was broken, like mine was.

I never got to see "up close and personal" what it looked like when spouses blessed each other in my home. My father bailed out when I was two months old and never came back. But I am incredibly grateful for God's Word and for godly people he put in my life who have shared and lived out the ideas and examples you'll read about in this book.

These thirty powerful ways to bless your husband can make a difference in your husband's life—as well as your own in the process—and if you have kids, can model for them what love, life, and blessing are all about. The blessing is something that can be given and experienced in small ways every day.

WHAT THE BLESSING IS

THE BLESSING IS about unconditional love and acceptance of a person. It is about

- ⭢ seeing the potential in someone,

- ⭢ assigning great value to that person,

- ⭢ reaching out with meaningful touch,

- ⭢ speaking words of blessing over them, and

- ⭢ demonstrating an active commitment to that person.

The blessing is for *all* relationships. Here we'll focus on specific ways that a wife can bless her husband. The relationship between husband and wife is one that is revered in Scripture. Husbands and wives are both instructed to put effort into their relationship. Marriage is to be protected and honored by those who believe in Jesus Christ, and it provides a picture of the sacrificial relationship between Jesus and his bride, the church.

The influence of a wife upon her husband is phenomenal. Will you be the kind of wife who builds her husband up and encourages him to be all that God created him to be?

I am so grateful to have an excellent wife. Cindy is my best friend, and she has stuck with me through thick, thin, and thinner. While neither of us grew up in a Christian home, we both were committed to establishing our marriage with Christ at the center and raising our family around the truth that Jesus is more precious than anything. Cindy has been a voice of wisdom for me through many career and personal decisions, and I would not be where I am today without her continual encouragement and support. Cindy believes in the blessing, and she has actively given me the blessing throughout the years of our relationship even when I've not been a model husband.

Having someone in our lives who believes in us and walks with us through life's challenges while cheering us on to be all that God created us to be can inspire us to pursue more than we might think is possible. I hope that your husband is that person for you and that you are that person for your husband.

A Culture of Blessing

Of course, giving of the blessing isn't just reserved for a once-in-a-lifetime momentous occasion. You can bless your husband in small ways every day! In fact, it's all these small, specific, positive ways you'll learn about that can help you as a wife create what we call a culture of the blessing in your home!

Think about a culture like setting a thermostat in your home. Try living in Chicago in February and setting the thermostat at 20 degrees throughout the house. No matter where you go in that home, the atmosphere, or culture, communicates one thing: it's cold! Your whole focus isn't on relating to others or being free to do things inside; your focus is on getting warm! But now set the thermostat at 72 degrees and watch life warm up and the focus of your family go from what's missing (heat) to all the things you *can do* as a family! You've added life (movement) to the home, because you've changed the thermostat (or culture)! And when you create a culture of blessing in the home, the entire family benefits. You all have the freedom to move towards God's best!

The Five Essential Elements

Let's get more specific on just what makes up the blessing. You'll see them pop up in the suggestions and examples that follow.

Throughout Scripture, five distinct elements usually characterized the blessing. First, the blessing began with a *meaningful touch*. The blessing continued with a *spoken message*, meaning the blessing was said or written out so it was unmistakable. The third element of the blessing was how the words always expressed *high value*. Fourth, the giver of the blessing pictured a *special future* for the one being blessed. And then these four attitudes and actions were lived out and demonstrated through an *active commitment* to see the blessing come to pass in that person's life.

Each of these five elements contributes its own impact on your blessing.

Meaningful Touch (Lovingly Touch)

A *meaningful touch* was an important part of giving the blessing in the Old Testament. When Isaac blessed his son, he called him, saying, "Come near and kiss me, my son" (Genesis 27:26, ESV). Isaac's words "come near" actually translate as "come and embrace in a bear hug." Jesus blessed the little children who came to him, "[taking] them in his arms and . . . laying his hands on them" (Mark 10:16, ESV). The benefits of touch are enormous—physically, emotionally, and spiritually. In marriage, meaningful touch is a primary means of communicating intimacy.

Research has shown, time and again, the incredible benefits of touch. For example, premature babies who are touched and held gain weight dramatically faster than those who aren't. (Touch isn't the reason why you or your husband has gained weight. Those studies on weight gain and touch only work with babies!) When someone puts their hands on another's shoulders—like you giving your husband a back rub—his blood pressure will go down, even if yours doesn't! Touch has many physical benefits, but perhaps most important, without a word being spoken, your touch is an incredibly powerful way to say, "I love you. I care for you."

Spoken Message (Say It!)

A *spoken message* has the power to build up or tear down a person's sense of worth. Our words hold great power, and the blessing acknowledges this through the spoken message. In the Bible, a blessing was invalid unless it was spoken. In the book of James, we see multiple pictures of the power of the tongue. The tongue is described as a bit that gives direction to a horse, a rudder that turns a ship, and a spreading fire (James 3:1–6). Each of these pictures shows us the potential of the tongue to build up or tear down. Will your tongue be one that encourages or belittles your husband? The apostle Paul challenged the church of Ephesus with these words: "Let no corrupting talk come out of your mouths, but only such as is good for building up, as fits the occasion, that it may give grace to those who hear" (Ephesians 4:29, ESV). Let your spoken words to your husband be words of blessing so that he may experience grace.

I remember one of my mentors, Dr. Howards Hendricks, once telling me about a counseling session he had that he never forgot. He had been trying to encourage a husband to be more verbally affirming with his wife. When he challenged him about the fact that he had never once said "I love you" to his wife since they got married over thirty years before, the man thundered at him from across the room, "I told my wife I loved her on the day we were married and it stands until I revoke it!"

That statement is wrong on so many levels! Just listen to the pride and anger dripping from those words. And the fact that at any time, his one-time statement could be withdrawn? Revoked? That man might have felt that his love still echoed after thirty plus years, but he was dead wrong. When you really love someone—even if you grew up not often hearing that love as a child or seeing your parents use loving words to encourage each other—you need to say it!

In the Scriptures, the word *love* occurs well over 300 times, and in fact, the Bible says that "God is love (1 John 4:8, 16). In the Gospel of John, we're told that "the Word became flesh and dwelt among us, and we have seen his glory, glory as of the only Son from the Father, full of grace and truth" (John 1:14, ESV). God didn't express his love just once. He sent his Son to embody his word, so we couldn't miss it! Just think about the fact that the only time the heavenly Father speaks to his Son on earth (at the baptism of Jesus and again at the Transfiguration),

PEOPLE WHO FEEL LOVED ARE HAPPIER AND THEY MAKE BETTER DECISIONS.

he says, "This is my beloved Son" (Matthew 3:17; 17:5). *Beloved!*

If anyone says to you, "Well, don't praise your husband or kids too much because they'll get a swelled head." Tell them the world is going to tell your husband and your kids in a hundred different ways that they're worthless and have no value. People who feel loved are happier and they make better decisions. It's best to praise your husband (or child) for persistence and their ability to stick with a difficult task, rather than intellect. Complementing their effort in the face of challenges is always good.

In fact, scientists have shown that applauding time, perseverance, and courage is better than praising intellect, attractiveness, or talent.

Wife, praising your husband works wonders—so say it!

In the book Song of Solomon, King Solomon's bride praises him twenty-four times in eight chapters. Your husband needs that same sort of encouragement and affirmation from you. He needs your blessing!

Attach High Value (Express High Value)

What kind of words are you to speak or write down for your spouse so that you might bless him? Those that *express high value*. To value something is to attach great importance to it. In blessing your spouse, you are choosing to ascribe great worth to him, acknowledging that he is valuable to the Lord and to you. This is important, even in times of conflict or struggle. Wife, your relationship with your husband will face times of great difficulty! But in the times when you may not feel the value of your spouse, choosing to speak words of high value to him will realign your own perspective and encourage him to see his value as well.

Remember, the word bless means to "bow the knee." I'll be telling you several suggestions for blessing your husband that won't cause your knees to ache, but they will help bring a deep sense of acceptance and appreciation as you express high value about who your husband is and how God has directed his life.

Picture a Special Future (See Potential)

With our *meaningful touch*, with our choice to use a *spoken message*, and by attaching words with *high value* to our spouse, we lay the foundation to help us picture a *special future* for them as well. As we attach value to a person, we can see their potential and envision the great ways in which they might impact the world for Christ. By paying attention to the strengths your husband exhibits, you can see how God might use his unique gifts to serve others and how his strengths might benefit his relationships and future endeavors. Encourage your spouse through picturing a special future for him in which God uses his gifts to impact others.

It's amazing how often and how well other people

can see something we're good at—or have potential in—when we just don't see it. Let me give you an example. There was a girl I went to grade school with. She had a beautiful older sister—a "stop traffic" older sister—who won every award at school. But Lynda, the girl I knew, was totally ignored. But then right at the end of high school, one person heard Lynda sing. And that person encouraged her by telling her that she had a really great voice. And the person talked her into taking singing lessons. And that led to her trying out for a talent show . . . and then trying out for a pageant . . . and that pageant led to the Miss Arizona pageant (which she won) . . . then to the Miss World pageant (where she reached the semi-finals) ... and then to television (where she eventually starred in her own program). You probably even know my grade-school friend, Lynda Carter, but you probably know her as Wonder Woman.

I knew Lynda pretty well in high school, but I marveled at the person she became when someone (not me) pointed out to her the potential she had to bless others with her singing.

Your husband needs you to tell him and give him a picture of the potential you see in him that can lead to a special future. OK, not necessarily winning a beauty pageant or starring in a television show. But his believing in his potential because he's heard it from you—that he could do more than he ever dreamed—if he just believed what you told him he could do. That God in him could do more than he could ever do by himself.

Later on you'll learn some practical ways to spot potential you can praise and help to develop in your husband (like a coach looking at a player and seeing who they can become). And you'll learn some ways you can demonstrate to your husband that you're here for the future, for the long haul. As far as you're concerned, the two of you will be together in the future no matter what and "as long as you both shall live." Seeing the potential in your husband is an amazingly powerful way of adding security and strength, vision and hope, energy and life to your husband. So get busy looking for and communicating ways you can encourage your husband's potential—that special future that he'll be sharing with you as the two of you hang together, forever!

Active Commitment (Be Committed)

The last element of the blessing really seals the deal, as the one giving the blessing demonstrates an *active commitment* to see the blessing come to pass in that person's life. Words have to be accompanied by action. The blessing is not merely spoken but lived—even when it's hard.

Wife, be intentional about connecting with and blessing your husband today. And as you do, you will be adding layer after layer of love and acceptance into his life that he'll be able to draw strength from when he faces challenges each and every day. The marriage relationship is under constant stress, but when you consistently strive to give your husband the blessing, you will work to create a culture of blessing within your marriage.

I live in Arizona, which is largely made up of desert. You may feel that your marriage is a desert—dry, hot, and maybe even exhausting! As you seek to give your husband the blessing and make your home and environment a culture of blessing, your marriage can become a tropical oasis rather than a desert. I am constantly challenging people to make small two-degree changes in their lives and watch as those changes impact the overall experience. You don't steer a huge cruise liner by jerking the steering wheel; gently turn the wheel in small increments and the direction (and destination!) of the boat is completely altered. In that same way, know that every small effort you make to bless your husband adds up to lasting impact in his heart.

Here's a way to remember all the various elements that make up the blessing—a way I teach to people, through an acronym: BLESS. While the elements are rearranged from the order in our discussion, this is an easy way to remember all five elements:

> **B** stands for "be committed" (active commitment)
>
> **L** stands for "lovingly touch" (meaningful touch)
>
> **E** stands for "express value" (high value)
>
> **S** stands for "see potential" (special future)
>
> **S** stands for "say it!" (spoken message)

You might consider posting this acronym on your fridge, bathroom mirror, or maybe by your desk computer—somewhere that you see regularly and can be reminded of your own desire to give the blessing to your husband. Use it as a tool to check up on yourself and evaluate how you are doing with each element.

Show-and-Tell

So now you know what the blessing is, why it's so important to choose to bless your husband's life, and what the basics are. The rest of the book is show-and-tell.

Any teacher knows that show-and-tell can be even more powerful than just tell. So in the pages that follow, I want to show you thirty simple, practical ways that wives have used to pass on the blessing to their husband.

You will see that each suggestion incorporates a variety of the five elements of the blessing. Some focus on using spoken words. Others incorporate a meaningful touch or help you to picture a special future. In some of the examples and occasions discussed, you'll see where all five come together in one activity or suggestion! And, yes, some aspects of each blessing might be easier for you to give than others. But the cumulative result of implementing all five elements of the blessing will help your husband in so many ways—emotionally, physically, spiritually.

I'm not asking you to try to force your way, by sheer willpower, to bless your husband. Rather, in freedom and drawing on your faith, start by just reading these ideas. Even just the first one. Then start adapting them in your own home. Try them out. Make up your own. Remember a way you were blessed or a way you saw your mother bless your father, and pass that on to your husband and speak it into his life.

Your goal isn't to try and mark a checklist as you use each example. Every attempt at passing on the blessing doesn't have to meet a list of must-do criteria. And there's no need to do each one perfectly. Nor does passing on a blessing have to result in the best evening ever or some huge emotional response from your husband. What you're looking to do is choose to layer in the blessing—to create that 72-degree culture of caring, acceptance, commitment, and courage in your home. It's not about perfection or emotion or doing something just right. It is about jumping in and going all in on being a wife who is going to choose to bless her husband.

And guess what will happen over time.

Over time, by choosing to bless your husband, you'll start creating that culture of blessing in your home. You'll see the blessing become a habit that enriches your home and eats discouragement and bad attitudes.

As you read these examples, they may bring back a memory of a time or way you saw your mother bless your father—with spoken or written words, by a gentle touch, by attaching high value to him, by picturing a special future for him, and by living out a life of genuine commitment.

YOU CAN TURN THINGS AROUND IN YOUR LIFE AND FAMILY!

Perhaps after you've read these, you'll pick a few that remind you of her. If she's living, take time to call her and tell her what a blessing her example was to you, and then get ready to bless your own husband.

But even if you didn't see the blessing happening

in your home growing up, *you can turn things around in your life and family!* Your words and actions can attach high value to your husband and say to him, "I'm crazy about you!"

Your husband deserves to know that you're crazy about him! Beyond that, your husband deserves to know that *Jesus* is crazy about him as well. It can change his life today and point him towards a special future tomorrow.

WHAT THE BLESSING DOES[1]

LET ME SHARE four reasons why the blessing can make a transformational change in your home.

The blessing defies a toxic culture.

The blessing runs full force against the tide of a busy society. With parents working long hours to make ends meet—or simply preoccupied with their own agendas—many children grow up today struggling with what experts call *attachment disorder*. That's the failure to create significant bonds in relationships. As adults, they stumble down the road in relationships with a deep desire for connection, but with the ever-present feeling that they just don't know how to build loving, lasting relationships. They step back from what they want most because they've never seen what it looks like to have someone step toward them.

Blessing your husband is about intentionally taking those steps—big and small—toward him. The blessing offers a way of reclaiming connection with your spouse, no matter how many hours the demands of our busy world try to siphon out of your day.

The blessing can help open a closed heart.

Christianity is about a relationship. When we trust in God, we enter into a relationship with our Creator. The blessing is all about building relationships! When you give your husband the blessing, you are helping him take hold of relational tools that can not only help him connect with you and other people, but can also open his heart to a new or strengthened relationship with Jesus.

The blessing can help free your spouse from a wounded past.

We all have good and bad in our past. Even adults who grew up in the best and most loving of homes might still carry with them a certain amount of hurt or disappointment.

Children don't have the maturity or understanding to deal with hurt and pain, so they develop self-protective mechanisms. They latch on to anything that they think can protect them and help them cope: athletic prowess, academic success, good looks, video games and social media, even drugs or alcohol. Whatever works, they want to repeat. By the time they grow up, they may have created layer upon layer of self-protection. But these layers have a shelf life! Success is fleeting. Looks fade. Addictive substances and activities don't satisfy deep longings.

> A HUSBAND WHO RECEIVES THE BLESSING CAN BE FREED TO PURSUE GOD'S BEST IN EVERY AREA OF HIS LIFE.

None of these self-protective mechanisms offer real, unshakable, lasting confidence and connection.

The blessing offers an alternative to damaging coping methods and the life-suffocating layers of self-protection. Instead of keeping himself wrapped in self-protection, a husband who receives the blessing can be freed to pursue God's best in every area of his life. What would it look like if your spouse didn't have to live in fear of not out-doing others at work? If he didn't have to worry about acquiring all the "toys" someone else has? If he could move beyond the issues that have held him back for years and finally make peace with his past? That can be another life-changing part of experiencing the blessing from God, from others, and from you.

The blessing is part of your calling.

Christians hear it from all corners today—from books, radio shows, websites, podcasts, and the pulpit. It's the call to a "sold-out" life of faith. It's the mission Jesus proclaimed for us: "Go therefore and make disciples" … everywhere! (Matthew 28:19, ESV).

But adopting this "missional" lifestyle that Christ called us to doesn't mean leaving your loved ones in the dust. Your family—your husband—is part of your calling. If you're not living out your faith and love for Christ with your family first, you have missed a huge first step!

If you find yourself too busy to give your husband the blessing because you're preoccupied with a "higher calling," you're missing the whole point of the gospel. The apostle Paul—a "missional" believer if there ever was one!—made it clear that "if anyone does not provide for his own, and especially for those of his household, he has denied the faith and is worse than an unbeliever" (1 Timothy 5:8). Building strong relational ties is part of your calling. The blessing can be one of your most important tools in ministering to your husband. And you just might find that your blessing will give him the confidence and encouragement to live a "sold-out" life for Christ along with you.

> **THE BLESSING CAN BE ONE OF YOUR MOST IMPORTANT TOOLS IN MINISTERING TO YOUR HUSBAND.**

Now that you have a grasp on what the blessing really is and why giving it to your husband is so important, let's jump into thirty ways to give the blessing to your husband.

30 WAYS TO BLESS YOUR HUSBAND

1

Love-the-Little-Things Blessing

Let me first start off by saying that you cannot tell your husband "I love you" enough times in a day.

One of the elements of the blessing is speaking words of high value. Say "I love you." Say it often! But take it further than that. Husbands love to be praised in concrete ways. So use your "I love you" words to praise your husband even more specifically. Even better, add some meaningful touch into the mix! For example, if your husband puts on cologne in the morning, hug him and tell him "I love the way that you smell. Thank you for making an effort to smell nice! I love you."

Acknowledge the little things that your husband does that you appreciate and/or are attractive to you. They can be as simple as the smell of cologne or as deep as the way you see him demonstrate an effort to lead your family spiritually. Here are a few ways to express your love for the little things your husband does:

- ⟲ "I love the way that you wear your hair."

- ⟲ "I love the way that you pray for our family before each meal."

- ⟲ "I love the way that you kiss me before you leave for work each day."

- ⟲ "I love the way that you do all you can to provide for our family."

- ⟲ "I love the way that you play with our kids."

➲ "I love the way that you sing in the shower."

➲ "I love the way that you remember my mother's birthday."

➲ "I love the way that you work to keep the lawn looking nice."

Add on specifics to each of your "I love yous." Pay attention to the little things (and the big things) that your husband does well, and point them out!

2

Love-Note Blessing

During one season of our marriage, I had to travel more often than normal. My precious awesome wife, Cindy, could have been really discouraged or allowed it to drive a wedge in our intimacy. I know at times I was discouraged and wished that I could be home instead of in another hotel. However, she did something that spoke life into our relationship and also gave me the support I needed to make it through the trip and get back home to her and the girls.

Cindy would write a love note and hide it somewhere in my suitcase while I was packing the night before a trip. Inevitably, I would find the note during the trip, often at a time when I needed encouragement. For Cindy, the note helped her to continue to take steps towards me in our relationship, even when it was a challenging season. For me, the words of blessing from my wife were a lifeline of encouragement and validation while I was away from her and our girls.

You don't have to write a whole letter, because even a simple note to your husband can make a big difference. Write your husband short notes and put them in places he will find them throughout his day. Stick one on the steering wheel of his car. Put one with his coffee mug. Place one in his briefcase. Hang one from his vanity mirror. Here are just a few one-liners you can write to your husband:

➲ "I'm proud of you."

➲ "You're the man of my dreams."

- "I know you will rock your presentation at work."

- "I'm praying for you."

- "God has great plans for you."

- "I can't wait until you are back home with me."

- "Excited to see you tonight!"

- "You are so good-looking."

- "Can't wait to see you!"

- "Excited about our plans this weekend!"

- "You're my favorite person!"

- "I'm thankful to be your wife."

Writing out words of blessing, words of high value, can be even more memorable than just hearing those words. Sometimes, something as simple as a sticky note with a few love-filled words on it can serve as a reminder of commitment like nothing else.

3

Hobby Blessing

 Cindy has made a special effort in our marriage to care about my hobbies and interests. She also does a great job of asking questions about things I'm interested in. For example, I'm a big baseball fan, and Cindy has taken the time to help me create a special keepsake display case in my home office with baseball memorabilia and other collector items I have. Cindy will occasionally sit with me while I watch a game, and during commercial breaks, she'll ask questions about stats, strategies, and players.

It is certainly healthy for husbands and wives to have a variety of interests. However, there is something powerful about a wife taking the initiative to be interested in the things her husband loves—even if she doesn't care greatly about them. Showing your husband that you care about what he enjoys and what is important to him goes a long way.

Check out these suggestions:

- ⟳ Does your husband love to hunt? Ask if he'll take you on a special hunting trip and teach you the basics. If you aren't sure you can stomach hunting, see if he'll take you to a shooting range and teach you how to shoot.

- ⟳ Is your husband a sports fan? Check out the game schedule for his favorite team. Get cheap tickets if you can or make arrangements to watch a game on TV with him. Before the game, ask him to give you an overview of the rules, if you don't know them. Or ask him to explain the referee's calls during the game (but maybe not every single one).

- ⟳ Does your husband enjoy grilling? Research some special marinades for him. Wrap up some grill tools for him as a surprise.

- ⟳ Is your husband the member of a gym? Or is he a runner? Make sure that he has the time necessary to get his regular exercise routine in by taking care of the kids during that time.

Ask him if you can run a noncompetitive 5K with him. Or sign up the family to participate together in a family fun run.

Whatever your husband is into, show him that you care about those things. Find ways to be both supportive and involved in what he loves.

4

Keep-Dreaming! Blessing

 In different seasons I've had different goals and dreams for specific areas of my life and family and with Cindy. My wife has been an incredible support as I've worked to finish my doctoral program, been employed as a youth pastor, and began writing, and as we both worked to get our girls through school and eventually college.

In each of those seasons of life, I've had different things that I've been excited about or struggled with. Cindy has done (and continues to do) a great job of helping me navigate the roadblocks that could have kept our family and me from achieving our dreams. A big reason Cindy is so great at encouraging me and identifying roadblocks is that she takes the time to figure out what my goals and dreams are (she's great at doing this with our girls too).

Do you know what your husband hopes for in his career? In your marriage? In your family? Ask him! Now, not every husband will be prepared to answer a loaded question like, "Where do you hope to see our family in ten years?" But asking him more manageable questions about his hopes and dreams can help him to share those things with you and allow you to encourage him. Consider starting with, "What are you hoping to accomplish at work this week? Is there any way I can help?" Or, "What's one thing you would like for our family to do this year? How can I help make that happen?"

God encourages us by saying, "For I know the plans I have for you, declares the LORD, plans for welfare and not for evil, to give you a future and a hope" (Jeremiah 29:11, ESV). You, the wife, can do the same thing for your husband. Let your husband know that his hopes and dreams for the future matter to you and that you want to do everything you can to help him see his dreams come true.

5

Man-Time Blessing

 For ten years, every Thursday morning at 6:00 a.m. I met with a few influential men in my life. We would spend the time being accountable, studying the Bible, and encouraging each other to be better men. This Thursday meeting threw off the weekly house routine for Cindy and the girls, but during the ten years that the group met, Cindy always made it a priority for me to be there. She would take on the role of both parents for a morning and even drive to school the carpool that I normally facilitated.

For me, that Thursday morning brought life, growth, and needed friendship with men who were pushing me to be a better man, dad, husband, and follower of Jesus.

It wasn't easy for Cindy to always make the time for me to be there on Thursday mornings, but she truly valued the importance of those relationships in my life and the growth that came from the meeting.

Does your husband have close friends? Are there men he talks about that he would like to get to know better? Make an effort for him to have time with other guys to build meaningful relationships. While meeting with other men for a weekly Bible study is a fine thing, there are a lot of other ways that your husband can be encouraged to build strong relationships with men who are going to help him build his faith walk and family life:

- Offer to make dinner and have the house clean for him and his buddies so that they can enjoy watching a ball game together.

- Encourage him to plan a guy's night out once a month.

- If he wants to join a Bible study or men's group, make it a priority for him to be at the meeting each time they get together.

➲ Even if his time with the guys is a weekly basketball game, work to make that a priority as well.

➲ Encourage him to plan a camping trip with some of the other fathers he's close to (or hopes to be close to), and take the kids away for a weekend (or maybe the wives can plan some girl time together while the husbands are away, if you can arrange for a trusted relative or friend to care for the kids).

➲ When time conflicts come up, instead of asking him to cancel guy time and watch the kids, get a babysitter lined up ahead of time. That alone shows him that you place high value on his relationships and the time he spends with his friends. When it's possible, change your plans so that your get-together takes place at your house, so you can be home to watch the kids.

The key for you as your husband pursues healthy relationships with other men is showing him that you value and encourage those relationships in his life. This not only gives him the freedom to enjoy those relationships but also allows him the needed accountability that other men can bring. Remember what Proverbs 27:17 has to say about being around good people: "Iron sharpens iron, and one man sharpens another" (Proverbs 27:17, ESV).

6

Stock-Your-Fridge Blessing

 Saturdays at our house are chore days. For me, the chore that I'm often tasked with is mowing the yard and making sure that all of the plants and trees are trimmed to perfection. Ten months out of the year, Arizona is an amazing place to live. But the two months of summer turn the outdoors into a raging inferno—similar to the feel of heat that rushes out when you open your oven when you're cooking something.

On those hot Saturdays, nothing is better than getting done with yard work, jumping in the pool, and then walking to the fridge and knowing that my favorite drink, iced tea, is there waiting for me.

The best part is, Cindy knows it's my favorite and has taken great care to make sure that if I'm doing yard work on Saturday, there will be an iced tea waiting for me when I'm done. This simple act of love speaks more to me in those moments than any pat on the back or "Good job, honey" could do.

There is a comfort in food that speaks to all of us! Here are some other ideas on how to bless your husband by keeping the fridge stocked:

- ⮕ Take note of what your husband loves to drink, and make sure to keep the fridge stocked with his favorite. Just making the effort to show him that you care in this way can be a blessing to him.

- ⮕ Keep his favorite snack on hand. Sometime you could even surprise him by having it ready to hand to him when he gets home from work or gets done with a hard task around the house.

➲ Ask him for a list of his four favorite meals. Make one meal each week throughout the month.

Homemade-or-Store-Bought Blessing

 Sometimes a homemade item means the most to us, and sometimes the effort taken to find a professional to create a special something makes the store-bought item more meaningful. Think about the occasions when it would be appropriate for you to make something for your husband to celebrate him, and think about the occasions when he might be thrilled by your effort to find a product made by a professional. Here are some ideas:

➲ If your husband always had store-bought birthday cakes growing up, make him a cake from scratch for his birthday. Or if he always had homemade cakes, find a specialty bakery and order him a cake. Instead of buying a Valentine's Day card for your husband, consider making him a card or writing him a letter. Write a blessing for him! You can include favorite memories from your history together, ways that you've seen him grow over the past year, things about him that you are proud of. Or visit a card store together and share your favorite cards with each other (you don't even have to buy them!).

- Make your husband a personalized photo frame with a casual snapshot of the two of you, or arrange for a professional photo shoot to capture a special occasion for the two of you (perhaps an anniversary).

- Purchase some of his favorite coffee syrup and make him a homemade latte, or take him out to a coffee shop that serves his favorite drink.

○ Decorate a mug (or order one with personalized engraving) that is exclusively for him to use at home.

As you study your husband, you will learn what items he will appreciate more if they are homemade or if they are purchased. Find ways to make things special for him and bless him through your thoughtfulness.

8

Least-Favorite-Chore Blessing

 Cindy and the girls can tell you that there is one chore around the house that makes me cringe inside. I don't mind cleaning bathrooms, washing the dogs, or even taking out the trash. But when it comes to watering the houseplants, I literally dread walking onto our back porch.

I don't have a green thumb, and over the years I have successfully overwatered and killed more houseplants than I would like to admit to.

One Saturday I headed out to water the plants and noticed that it was already done. Cindy had gotten up early and decided to bless me by watering them. Knowing that task was done for the day made it one of the happiest Saturdays I'd had in a while.

It may sound silly, but Cindy saw how much it blessed me to have that chore taken off my plate. From then on out, either she or the girls officially took on watering the plants. This not only blessed me but saved the lives of a multitude of houseplants (and, incidentally, it saved our budget from being depleted because we had to replace them).

While I'm not saying you need to permanently take over doing a chore that is particularly stressful for your husband, there are ways to bless him and encourage him to make the chore a blessing:

- Is there a chore that your husband does regularly? Maybe taking out the trash? Having the car serviced? Surprise your husband by taking care of a chore for him.

- Encourage him to invite a friend over to help with a specific project.

- Have his favorite drink and snack ready for him when he's done.

- Change up the chore list, and add something fun like "play catch with the kids."

Throughout the week, look for ways to serve and bless your husband by doing one or two of his chores, especially if you know he's stressed at work or is having a busy week.

9

Goodnight-Kiss Blessing

 When Cindy and I first got married, we would always go to bed at the same time. After thirty-seven years, we still try to go to bed at the same time whenever possible. This gives us a few moments together—without the kids or stress of the day—to bless one another and to address any issues that have come up during the day that we haven't already discussed.

As often as you can, I would encourage you to go to bed at the same time as your spouse. Turning in for the night together will give you a regular opportunity to talk and reconnect with each other after the busyness of the day.

Another thing I would encourage you to do is faithfully kiss your husband good night.

If you are resistant to the idea of kissing your husband good night on any given night, deal with whatever the issue is right then! If you make this a habit every night, you are much more likely to head off any major conflicts between the two of you.

You and your husband are a team, and when you kiss him good night, you let him know that you are committed to him.

I'd encourage you to start the day with a kiss as well. Every reminder that you can give your husband that you have his back and that he has your love from the very start of the day until the end of the day is a blessing that will make a big difference in the long-term intimacy of your marriage.

10

Habits-of-Touch Blessing

Cindy does a great job of incorporating meaningful touch into daily conversations. Even in a tense conversation, she grabs my hand and does a great job letting me know that she values me.

For some people, meaningful touch is the biggest way that they receive love. They need that type of affirmation. A hug. Holding hands. Even if it's just for a minute, that touch makes all the difference in the world to them.

Even if touch isn't your spouse's main way of receiving love, it is still an important part of any relationship, and it is a key to continuing intimacy.

If meaningful touch doesn't come completely naturally to you, there are a few things you can do to incorporate it into your marriage:

➲ Grab his hand when you're walking to the car.

- Make a dozen coupons for your husband to redeem anytime he wants a massage from you. Keep some massage oil or lotion on hand for when he turns in a coupon.

- Give him a hug before he leaves for work in the morning and when he gets home at night. Encourage the kids to do the same.

- Put your hand on his shoulder or grab his hand when he shares with you.

Another secret to meaningful touch comes straight from Proverbs 15:30: "The light of the eyes rejoices the heart" (ESV). While the eyes and heart may not seem connected, when your eyes and face light up—especially in conjunction with physical touch—the impact runs deep. Next time you grab your husband's hand, try looking at him with bright eyes. This will add even more affirmation and blessing to your touch and will bless his heart.

11

Prayer Blessing

A Gallup poll shared some staggering statistics about couples and prayer. The results showed that while the divorce rate may still be 50 percent among Christian couples, those couples who chose to pray together on a daily basis stayed married. In fact, less than 1 percent of those couples who prayed together ended up getting a divorce.

It's safe to say that those couples who pray together, stay together.

Prayer is also an incredible way to encourage your husband and fight for him, even when you can't be in the boardroom at his work or with him when he coaches the Little League team. Prayer is an incredibly powerful way to partner with your husband as well as keep your heart for your husband.

When you pray for your spouse, you will begin to change. You will begin to see your husband in different ways; and instead of looking at the negatives, you'll begin to find ways to pray for and encourage him. You will also feel more connected to him and to what is going on in his life.

Cindy and I pray each night before we go to bed. When the girls were living at home, we would all stand around whoever was going to bed first and pray as a family.

Prayer doesn't have to be overwhelming or time consuming. You can use it as a quick check-in on a regular basis with your husband about what lies ahead in his schedule. Pray for the meetings, presentations, or other important events he has coming up at work. Keep track of the days that he has something big going on, and take a moment before he leaves in the morning to say a prayer over him.

If you are still struggling with how to use prayer as a blessing, here are some simple ways to add it into your marriage and family:

⮑ Set an alarm, and when the alarm goes off, stop and say a quick twenty-second prayer for whatever is happening at that time. This is also a great way to not just say, "I'll be praying for you" but to back it up as well. Cindy and I would set an alarm to go off before a big meeting or big test for the girls at school.

⮑ Make a list of all the things you are praying about for your husband and put it someplace handy (like in your cell phone, if your phone has an app for that). You can change it weekly, and it can list everything from short-term needs to long-term dreams and/or goals. Having it written down makes it easy to pray when you are waiting to pick up the kids, are stuck in line at the grocery store, or even have a few minutes in between work meetings.

Always remember that "the prayer of a righteous person has great power as it is working" (James 5:16, ESV).

12

Relive-Your-Wedding Blessing

 Cindy and I love to look back at our old wedding album. While wedding videos weren't a "thing" when we got married, we both get a kick out of the photos and memories of that incredible day. And our girls love making fun of my big hair and dead tooth. Cindy laughs at the gray suits that I picked out for the groomsmen, which I still claim were way ahead of their time. As we look through the photos together, we share stories about different family members and the funny things that happened leading up to that day.

Every time we look at the album I always end up getting choked up, from looking at Cindy that day and looking at our life now. It's amazing how full life has been and how much God has blessed us. Taking the time to remember special moments and look back has an incredible way of providing a different perspective on the current challenges and stresses.

You can even take this a step beyond your wedding album and have a picnic on the living room floor with your husband. Have the TV set up to run a loop of photos from your entire time together. Take time to laugh and remember fun and special moments that you've had together. It's not only a cheap date night, but the memories and blessings of taking time to celebrate where you are and where you have been are also incredibly powerful.

Reminisce with your husband about the day you got married. Talk about what you loved about that special day. Look through your wedding album or watch your wedding video together. Read your vows together. Encourage your husband with how you have seen him uphold his vows. Affirm for him the reasons that you married him and the joy you find in still being married to him today.

13

Favorite-Dish Blessing

Men love food. It's a fact.

Cindy and my girls laugh because if you ask them what my favorite time in the world is, they will all answer in unison "on vacation, with our family, at a restaurant, eating dinner."

There is something so special about eating my favorite meal with my family.

Even though we're empty nesters, Cindy continues to bless me by either making my favorite meal or taking me out to eat at my favorite restaurant.

Is there any better way to a man's heart than through his stomach? Maybe cooking isn't your forte, but even if it isn't, making an effort to learn to cook what your husband really enjoys can go a long way. You don't have to master every sort of cuisine, but making a concentrated effort to prepare at least one dish that your husband loves can show him that you care about him.

14

Unplugged Blessing

 Cindy and I have always had the same rule: "We don't answer the phone at the dinner table." Even before the world was invaded by cell phones, Cindy and I would make sure that we protected dinnertime and family time from the interruptions of technology.

We live in a culture that is hyperconnected, and sadly, our social-media-driven society can influence our relationships negatively. There is a lure to always stay in touch with everyone at all times. Unfortunately, this can make the people right in front of us feel less important than our phones, and those people may end up being the ones disconnected from us.

Laptops, tablets, cell phones—all of these things can be incredible blessings, but they can also subtract from the face-to-face interaction that your husband needs in your relationship. Set boundaries on your media intake while you are with your husband. Put your phone away during the evening hours that you have together. Shut down the screens, and work to ensure that the time you spend together is personal time together, instead of technology-oriented. Connection happens in person. Too many of us have been at a dinner table or in a meeting with someone who couldn't look up from their phone long enough to really talk to us.

Don't leave your husband feeling like he is second to your Twitter following or Facebook friends. You won't regret spending those moments technology-free and engaging in real connection and conversation with your husband. Those Facebook photos or Pinterest finds will still be there tomorrow, and you and your husband will benefit from the time spent building intimacy rather than a social-media following.

15

Choice-Picture Blessing

 Pictures have a way of sticking in our minds like nothing else. Pictures evoke emotions and memories. They capture moments from a unique perspective.

Do you keep a picture of your husband in a prominent place? Keeping as the wallpaper background on your computer and your smart phone a picture of your husband or of you and your husband together can communicate to your husband that he is the most important person in your life and that you enjoy seeing his face, even when he is not around!

As you take family pictures through the years, I would encourage you to continually capture pictures of just you and your husband—without the kids.

Often as families grow, the desire to capture every moment of the children's lives usurps the relationship of the husband and wife (at least in photos). I know some couples that would struggle to find a picture of just themselves without their children that wasn't from before their children were born.

Cindy doesn't have a smart phone, but she did take my favorite picture of just the two of us from last Christmas and put a framed copy of it on her desk at work.

Remember that your husband will be the one who is with you, even after the kids have left the nest. Show your husband that you love and treasure him by giving him the spotlight, even above your children.

16

Date-Night Blessing

 From very early on in our marriage, Cindy and I have gone on a weekly date night. When our daughters were young, we would pay a babysitter once a week to watch

the girls while we went to the mall, picked a table in the food court, and sat and talked. We would each share about something we felt was going really well in our relationship and something we felt we needed to work on as a couple. Cindy was committed to making sure date night happened every week.

Carve out time to date your husband. Dating shouldn't stop when you're married! I'm not saying you have to go to a fancy restaurant or even leave the house, but you should make an effort to spend some designated time together—just the two of you. Bless your husband by demonstrating a genuine interest in what is going on in his mind and heart and finding out how you might support him in his endeavors. Here are some ideas you don't even have to leave your house to make happen. Once the kids are put to bed, spend thirty minutes (or more) *together* doing one of the following:

- Playing a board game

- Baking cookies together

- Playing a game of Twister

- Planning a dream vacation

- Sharing a favorite snack or dessert

- Setting goals for the week

- Watching a show

- Reading a chapter of Scripture

- Looking at a family photo album

- Watching home videos

- Taking silly pictures

- Stargazing in your backyard

- Working on a home project

- Doing a crossword puzzle

- Listening to a radio show

- Picking three questions to ask each other while having a cup of coffee or tea

Dating your husband doesn't have to break the bank. Often the simplest times together are the most memorable and bring the greatest blessing. Protecting your time together is important and will bless your husband in great ways.

Bragging Blessing

If I were to ask your best friend what kind of man your husband is, what would be her answer? Would she struggle to say something positive, because all she hears from you are complaints about him? Would she have an honorable view of him? Marriage can be tough, and I'm not saying that there aren't appropriate times to share struggles with those who give godly counsel. However, the way you speak about your husband to your friends matters. Instead of always pointing out the negatives, make an intentional effort to tell your friends positive things about your husband. Speak words of high value about him to others.

In the book Song of Solomon in the Bible, the woman highly praises her husband to others, and when they ask her what sets apart her husband from the rest, she answers with lengthy praise. I really love how she describes him as being "distinguished among ten thousand" (Song of Solomon 5:10, ESV). This woman knows what speaking words of high value about her husband means, and she speaks those words freely to her friends.

I always know that Cindy has spoken positively about me to others when she introduces me to someone (or kindly says, "John, you remember Elaine?" [because most likely I've forgotten her name]) and the other person responds, "So nice to see you. Cindy has told me that you have been busy speaking and encouraging lots of parents. I know she is thrilled to have you home right now." Cindy has plenty of opportunities to be frustrated with me, but she chooses to express the joy in our relationship to her friends.

In-Law Blessing

I know it can be a challenge for many women to fully embrace their husband's family. But I also know that it blesses your husband when you honor his family. It may be that your husband's family is dysfunctional, and he doesn't really desire to be part of it. If that's the case, honor him first, but also make an effort to speak positively about his family as much as possible, searching for redeeming qualities wherever they might be hiding. Conversely, your husband may have a close-knit family that he loves being a part of. Find ways to honor them. Remember their birthdays. Invite them to participate in meaningful events in your family's life. Include them in the lives of your children. There are certainly appropriate boundaries that you and your husband can work to establish with both your family and his, but do all that you can to establish and maintain harmonious relationships with your in-laws. It will bless your husband to see that you care to build positive relationships with other people who he loves.

Cindy has worked to have positive relationships with my family, even though we have plenty of issues. She reminds me of my brothers' birthdays (even that of my twin!) and makes sure that we celebrate them and invite them to be part of many of our family celebrations. Cindy even made an effort to honor and share Christ with my father, who was absent for the majority of my childhood.

Paul said that we should "if possible, so far as it depends on you, live peaceably with all" (Romans 12:18, ESV). Doing all you can to have positive relationships with your in-laws will bless your husband. You can be sure of it.

Bite-Your-Tongue Blessing

I know a young couple who has a great tradition of every year on their anniversary, making a list of ten things that they find attractive in their spouse and two things about their spouse that they find irritating. For a couple of years, the husband would write that his wife correcting him in conversations with others was aggravating to him. Why? Because the husband felt disrespected. The issue was not that the husband never believed he was wrong, but having his wife correct minor or nonessential details in a conversation with other people made him feel as if his wife didn't support and respect him, and he thought that it made him look foolish to other people.

Maybe you have a similar tendency to correct your husband. Making an effort to bite your tongue when he is telling a story or talking with others is a way that you can communicate respect for him and, in so doing, bless him. This doesn't mean that you should never correct your husband, but the timing and attitude of your correction are important. You don't want to undermine him with other people or with your children. Don't be your husband's critic. Be his fan. Appreciate the way he tells a story. Be careful not to interrupt him. Even if others aren't listening, let him know that he always has a captive audience with you.

T-Shirt Blessing

I don't know anyone who doesn't love a free T-shirt, men included. Does your husband like humorous T-shirts? Make him a shirt that says "I'm Taken" or "I Liked It, So I Put A Ring On It" underneath a wedding picture of the two of you or even stick figures representing the two of you. Get creative in making a keepsake T-shirt that he can wear to show that you are proud that he is your husband. You can even make the two of you shirts that go together. You could have one shirt read "My Wife Thinks I'm Awesome" and the matching shirt could read "My Husband Thinks I'm Awesome." Use a T-shirt to attach high value to your husband in a way that he can display to others.

21

Photo-Booth Blessing

When's the last time you took photos in a photo booth? There's something exciting about spontaneously coming up with poses as the timer counts down and takes several snapshots in a small booth with a small curtain blocking out the hustle and bustle around you. Photo booths are just fun. Next time you are passing one, coax your husband in and try to come up with the silliest poses you can in the short time you're allotted. Post the photo strip on the fridge at home. After it's been there a while, stick it somewhere that your husband will find it—make it into a bookmark, stick it in the sun visor of his car, or tuck it in the checkbook next to the next blank check.

22

Texting Blessing

The words "I miss you" carry such value in them. To miss something means that that something matters to you, that you enjoy it, that you treasure it. To miss someone says all of that—and more. There may be times in your marriage where you and your husband have longer periods of separation due to business trips or other life circumstances. Those may be times when it is easy to say "I miss you" to your husband. But do you ever tell him you miss him over the course of a regular workday? Do you let your husband know that you enjoy his company and look forward to seeing him at the end of each day? Let your husband know that you are thinking about him during the day. Send him a short text letting him know that you miss him.

— **23** —

Two-Questions Blessing

There are two simple questions you can ask your husband to show that you value him. First, regularly ask your husband, "What do you think?" It means a lot to have someone ask for your opinion. Your husband isn't beyond this. Oftentimes husbands can feel like their wives have it all together and their husband's thoughts don't matter to them. Even asking about simple things can communicate that your husband's view is important to you:

- ➲ "What do you think about the issue I'm having with my boss?"

- ➲ "What do you think we can do to help our kids get along better?"

- "What do you think would be best for us to do this weekend?"

- "What do you think about this dress?"

Ask your husband what he thinks, and listen to what he says. Show that you care about his opinion about minor and major issues.

The second question to ask your husband is, "Would you help me with this?" Every man desires to be needed. I'm not saying you should have a running list of things that you constantly nag your husband to do, but asking your husband for help shows him that you want his support in even the most mundane tasks of life:

- "Would you help me by loading the dishwasher while I get the kids ready for bed?"

- "Would you help me with thinking through some career decisions I have to make?"

- "Would you help me with bringing in the groceries?"

- "Would you help me with making plans with our families for the holidays?"

Don't forget to thank your husband when he answers your requests for help. Appreciate him and let him know you value his contributions. Bless him by seeking out his opinion and his help and thanking him for what he does.

—— **24** ——

Budget Blessing

 Are you and your husband on the same page about your finances? Money can be one of the greatest conflicts in marriage. If you don't have a budget, spend some time making one with your husband. You can find free budget worksheets online to get you started. Decide who will be responsible for various categories of the budget, and work hard to stay within the limits you designate for the categories you assume responsibility for. If you're struggling to stay within the budget you set together, talk to your husband. Ask him for help. Work to create open communication between the

two of you about money, trusting God to "supply every need of yours according to his riches in glory in Christ Jesus" (Philippians 4:19, ESV). If you're anxious, ask your husband to pray with you about the situation.

— —

Forgiveness Blessing

 Your husband is someone who you will live with through life's ups and downs, which includes his ups and downs. There will be times that you deeply struggle to forgive the words he speaks to you in anger, the neglect he demonstrates for a task you have asked him to do, the quick dismissal of your feelings about an issue. But blessing someone isn't just about loving them when everything is peachy. It's about loving unconditionally. It's about demonstrating genuine acceptance, even when that person is living out their weaknesses.

It's important to forgive your husband. Forgiveness is vital in a healthy marriage. I cannot tell you how many times I have counseled couples who struggle with forgiving one another. When you allow grudges against one another to develop, your marriage will suffer; distrust and anger will begin taking root in your marriage. I know a couple who struggled with remaining sexually abstinent before marriage. The man was convicted of the sin in their relationship and apologized to his then-girlfriend for his failure to lead in this part of the relationship and honor her. The woman forgave him, and they made a commitment to each other to wait from that point on until they were married to allow their relationship to be physical. Not long after they made this commitment, the woman found out she was pregnant. Though they went through some difficult times, the couple married and welcomed a baby boy into the world not long after. The woman said that learning to forgive one another, even before they were married, was one of the greatest foundations of their relationship. She explained that while many couples go through a honeymoon period at the beginning of their marriage and then experience a decline in the superficial feelings that many experience early in a relationship, she and her husband started at rock bottom, and in many ways, they had nowhere to go but up.

At the same time, sometimes love means not allowing someone to be self-destructive or to deliberately do wrong or to spin out of control. Sometimes a call to a professional is the best way you can love your husband.

Never forget that we are admonished to always "be kind to one another, tenderhearted, forgiving one another, as God in Christ forgave [us]" (Ephesians 4:32, ESV).

26

Hand-Holding Blessing

 Do you remember the first time you and your husband held hands? Often, in public, if you see a couple holding hands, the assumption is that they are dating rather than

married. Do you hold your husband's hand when you are in public together? Did hand holding fade into the background after you and your husband said "I do" to each other? Bring hand holding back into the spotlight! Holding hands is a way to bless your husband through meaningful touch. By holding your husband's hand, you can communicate to your husband that you are glad to be identified with him. You're proud of him. You enjoy him.

I know a couple who have a tradition that after every mealtime prayer together, they give each other a kiss. No matter who they are dining with! They make a conscious effort to infuse their relationship with meaningful touch by creating a pattern in their lives. Researchers have found that even a small hug in the morning and evening, even if you're only half awake or your mind is on something else, makes a significant difference in a marriage. Create a pattern in your life to bless your husband through meaningful touch, starting with holding his hand.

27

Laughing Blessing

 Do you and your husband have a good sense of humor? Do you ever play jokes on each other? Do you ever listen to or watch comedies together? Do you send each other funny YouTube videos? Do you share funny moments from your day with each other? Finding ways to laugh with your husband will bring great blessing to your marriage and to him.

I know a couple who has been through a lot—and I mean a lot. They adopted several children out of foster care, some with deep emotional issues, in addition to having biological children. They have gone through therapy after therapy trying to stabilize the relationships between all of the children. What's more, the husband went through a health crisis and ended up being hospitalized for more than forty days. So it is safe to say, this family has been through some serious trauma, yet the wife continually has sought to bless her husband throughout each and every trial they faced. One thing she shared with me when they once were really struggling with the kids was that every evening after the kids were in bed, she and her husband would clean the kitchen together while listening to their favorite stand-up comedian. They always sought to end the day—no matter how tough it had been—laughing together. They faced days that were no laughing matter, but they knew that laughter was important in maintaining their camaraderie—their fellowship, their friendliness, their togetherness—through all of life's challenges. The wife was committed to blessing her husband in this way, and it was a large reason why they always seemed to be on the same page through each crisis that came their way.

As it says in Proverbs, "A joyful heart is good medicine, but a crushed spirit dries up the bones" (Proverbs 17:22, ESV). Find a way to bless your husband through laughter. You won't regret it.

28

Read-Aloud Blessing

 When I was young, academics were not my thing. I was the "problem" child at school— the one who wouldn't focus or stay on task. But my mother believed in me. And who knew that years later I would have a PhD!

Reading is something that I believe inspires and challenges us in a way like no other. Choosing to read together with your husband will give you a shared experience that encourages both of you.

If there's an area in your relationship that you feel can use some work on it, ask your husband if you two can read a book about it. Take turns reading out loud to each other. Talk about each chapter and reflect on what you agree and disagree with in the text. Seek out wisdom together.

Reading a book with your husband can provide a unique way for the two of you to connect. It can also create opportunities for conversations that you might not otherwise have, and it can allow you to express appreciation for your husband as you learn together.

29

Friendship Blessing

 For years, Cindy and I helped to lead a couples class at our home church in Scottsdale. The experience was not just for us to impart great wisdom to others but also to build camaraderie with other couples. Cindy was committed to us being part of the class as much as we were able. Even on weeks that I was traveling, she made a special effort to attend herself and maintain the friendships that we had in the class. She saw the value of us not going through our marriage in isolation but surrounding ourselves with other couples who were walking through the ups and downs of marriage as well.

Make an effort to build relationships with other couples that you can walk through life with. It will be a blessing to your husband. Here are some simple ideas of how to get to know other couples:

- ⟲ Invite a couple over for a meal on the weekend.

- ⟲ Plan a date night out with just a few couples. Share a babysitter!

- ⟲ Join a couples Bible study.

- ⟲ Go to a marriage conference together and make it a goal to meet at least three couples and exchange contact information.

- ⟲ Make your children's birthday parties family events where the adults are included, and get to know the kids' parents.

- ⟲ Host a couples game night at your house and play games that encourage conversation.

Life can get busy, but making an effort to do life with others will be a blessing to your husband and your relationship.

30

Word-Picture Blessing

 I believe one of the most powerful ways to communicate in relationships is through the use of emotional word pictures. In fact, Gary Smalley and I wrote an entire book, *The Language of Love*, on using emotional word pictures. I want to encourage you to use an emotional word picture to bless your husband. Obviously, this requires some understanding of what an emotional word picture is and how to create and use one effectively.

Emotional word pictures are not a new idea. Leaders throughout history have used emotional word pictures to enrich their communication with a variety of audiences. We even see many emotional word pictures used throughout Scripture. An excellent example is described in 2 Samuel 12, when the prophet Nathan paid a visit to King David. Nathan told David a story of a rich man and a poor man. The rich man had many herds of sheep and access to all sorts of luxuries and resources. The poor man, on the other hand, had only one lamb that he cared for with great tenderness. Nathan explained that the rich man was visited by a guest, and in choosing what to prepare for dinner for the guest, he had the poor man's lamb slaughtered. When David heard the story, he was outraged at the rich man and exclaimed that the rich man would be severely punished for his wrongdoing. Nathan then pointed to David and said that David was the rich man, and the lamb had been another man's wife (Bathsheba), who David had selfishly taken for himself. David was struck to the heart at Nathan's words. Nathan had effectively used an emotional word picture to communicate a difficult truth to David.

An emotional word picture is a communication tool that uses a story or object to stimulate both the emotions and intellect of a person. Because of this, rather than simply hearing words spoken, the listener actually experiences our words. Word pictures hold the potential to maximize the impact of what we want to communicate to another person. While in the instance of Nathan and David, a word picture was used to gently but powerfully point out a flaw within David, word pictures can be used to convey positive feelings in an impactful way as well. That being the case, emotional word pictures are an incredible way to bless your spouse!

Let's walk through some steps for creating an emotional word picture:

1. *Clarify your purpose*—For this discussion, we will focus on praising your husband through an emotional word picture.

2. *Become very familiar with your husband's interests*—In the case of Nathan and David, the emotional word picture was so powerful because it drew from David's experience as a leader and a shepherd. Knowing the interests and experiences of your spouse will enable you to create a significant emotional word picture.

3. *Take advantage of the inexhaustible wells of word pictures*—You may be intimidated by the prospect of creating an emotional word picture, but there are several "wells" of examples that you can draw from:

- ⮞ Nature—Think about experiences you have had personally in nature, scenes that evoke certain emotions in you, etc.

- ⮞ Everyday objects—Consider the purpose of various objects you use on a regular basis, things that may hold sentimental value to you, items that you attribute desirable characteristics to, etc.

- ⮞ Imaginary stories—Think about scenes from your favorite movies, characters from classic books, etc.

- ⮞ Past experiences—Recall happy shared events and.

4. *Practice, practice, practice*—An effective emotional word picture is rehearsed so that the story is clear and the meaning will be better understood.

5. *Choose your timing wisely*—When you deliver your emotional word picture, you want your husband to be free of distractions.

6. *Don't give up*—Not every word picture is effective the first time, but building on your story will increase the effect over time.

7. *Dive deeper and deeper into your word picture*—The more details you can add to your word picture, the more powerful the word picture will be.

As you create a word picture for your husband, make sure you have some examples to get you going. Read over the following great word pictures that have been used by wives to bless their husbands. You may find one that you can use just as it is, or you may find the inspiration you need to create a completely unique word picture for your husband.[2]

➲ My husband treats me like a roomful of priceless antiques. He walks in, picks me up, and holds me with great care and tenderness. I often feel like I'm the most precious thing in our home. He saves the best hours and his best effort for me, not the television.

➲ I'm a ship with brightly painted banners riding the warm, gentle, Caribbean breeze of my husband's love. All through my childhood, I was forced into an unsafe ship and made to ride across the North Atlantic. I was nearly shipwrecked more times than I could count. But with my husband's love, I feel like I've traded ships and sailed around the world. Instead of the fierce gales of the Atlantic, I feel like there's always a steady warm trade wind blowing me to a safe harbor.

There have been times over the years when I've faced hailstorms that I thought would turn into tornadoes. But like the shelter of a storm cellar, I can always run to my husband to protect me from hardship. He's as solid as a rock, and I know he'll always be there when the storm clouds blow into my life.

I love my husband because he always makes sure I know I'm the number one woman in his life. He reminds me of a beautiful English setter. His amber coat glows as he romps in the meadow near our house. I know there are other dogs in the meadow—beautiful show dogs, far prettier than I. But he always ignores them and comes back to me. His soft brown eyes tell me each night, "There is no one but you."

- Marrying you was like getting a release from life's prison of loneliness. For thirty-six years, I spent every night in solitary confinement. I now spend each night in a garden of love, with the one I love sleeping next to me.

- Though I'm just like millions of other women, when I'm with you I feel like a prize painting hanging in a place of honor in a lovely mansion. I'm the object of your undivided attention and the admiration of all who enter the room—all because you treat me like a priceless work of art.

- When I think of our marriage, I feel like Cinderella. Never in my wildest dreams did I think you'd ever want me. Yet the slipper fit. And life with you, my Prince Charming, has been all I envisioned in my little girl dreams!

From these examples, I hope you have gotten some inspiration for an emotional word picture you might develop and bless your husband with. The possibilities are endless, and using an emotional word picture allows you to bless your husband in a very unique and personal way.

WHY CHOOSE TO BLESS

THE CHOICE YOU make to bless your husband, even in small ways, can be life-giving and life-changing for both of you. This is particularly true if one or both of you didn't receive or see the blessing while growing up.

Life over Death, Blessing over Curse

In Deuteronomy, the Lord says to his people, "I call heaven and earth to witness against you today, that I have set before you life and death, blessing and curse. Therefore choose life, that you and your offspring may live" (Deuteronomy 30:19, ESV). That's one choice with two parts: (1) life over death, and (2) blessing over curse. In Scripture the word *life* means movement; things that are alive are moving towards someone or something. The word *death* means to step away. That's a word picture of your first choice as a wife.

Are you going to step towards your husband—with appropriate touch, with spoken words that attach high value, by picturing a special future for him and showing him your genuine commitment? Or are you going to choose to step away—because of work, because you just don't know how to bless him, or because you never saw your mother bless your father?

Know this: what keeps us choosing to step towards our spouse is having made that first foundational choice for life in Christ! When we choose life in him, Jesus tells us, "I came that [you] may have life and have it abundantly" (John 10:10, ESV). That's LIFE in all capitals!

So when you choose Jesus as your Lord and Savior—that foundational, empowering, life-changing choice—you start moving towards his best! The new life Jesus gives you when you choose him gets you moving towards godly things—towards being more like Jesus each day, towards others in service, love, and commitment! The abundant life he offers gives you his power and strength to keep moving towards your spouse in a positive way—even on those days (or seasons) when it's tough or difficult to do so or when you really feel like stepping away. Even if you yourself never got the blessing or saw the blessing being given growing up, you can change the pictures of your life story! Jesus gets you unstuck and moving towards him—and towards others!

So are you going to step towards or step away from the Lord? To step towards or away from your spouse? If you choose to step away from your spouse, instead of moving towards him, on an earthly level, you'll see your marriage start dying by degrees.

I see this every day in my counseling practice. My day job is being the Gary D. Chapman Chair of Marriage and Family Ministry and Therapy at Moody Theological Seminary. That's a very long title, but what it means is that I get to counsel couples and train counselors who can help couples make that choice for life in Jesus and get moving towards each other.

I feel I have the best job on the planet, but the most challenging thing I see each day are those awesome couples who started out stepping towards the Lord and towards each other, but then something happened. One spouse felt offended by something the other said or did, and slowly, but then more quickly, one spouse decides to start emotionally—and soon physically—stepping away from the other. And if that couple continues heading down that path, they'll wake up one day to find that they've quit looking for light and love from the source of life and are "suddenly" miles away from each other emotionally. They'll find that they're like the church of Ephesus described in Revelation: "[They] abandoned the love [they] had at first" (Revelation 2:4, ESV).

A Way Back

So what if your marriage has deteriorated to the point where you wonder if there's anything left? There is a way back to happiness and wholeness in marriage. There's a biblical path your family can walk that leads you towards fulfillment, love, and peace. It's the way of blessing—small actions like the thirty examples you've read that you can draw on to communicate genuine love and acceptance to your husband; small actions that add up to big results.

Two Word Pictures

In Scripture, the Hebrew word for *to bless* suggests two pictures. The first picture is that of bowing the knee. This doesn't mean you have to bow literally to your spouse! That would be a little strange and confusing! But it's a picture of your acknowledging—which bowing did in olden times and still does in some cultures—that you are in the presence of someone who's extremely valuable. In this case, it's your spouse who you've chosen to bless.

With the hundreds of couples I've sat with over the last forty years, I have yet to meet with one who didn't start off thinking the other person had great worth and value. Yes, love can be blind, but the feeling they had was "this person is nothing short of great." And that's a great starting point!

When the church at Ephesus headed off in the wrong direction and drifted away from their first love for Jesus, he called them back: "Remember therefore from where you have fallen" (Revelation 2:5, ESV). He didn't say, "OK, spend all your time thinking about the lowest point in your relationship with me." His advice on how to rebuild and regain what they'd lost wasn't to focus on their failures or their disappointments. Instead, Jesus called them back to when they valued him highly: "Remember from where you've fallen." In other words, "Remember when you were looking up!"

You don't fall from the lowest point in your life! Jesus tells us to look up and remember when things were at their best—when we were on the right road! When we were choosing to bless our spouse, almost without trying, because we felt so strongly that this person was someone of great worth and value! And if you feel like that's not where you are today, keep this in mind: actions dictate feelings—not the reverse.

In other words, when you choose to act like someone has great worth or value—like you did when you first married—you will find your *feelings* for them will begin to follow. But never the reverse. If you just sit and wait until you feel like blessing or valuing your husband, get ready for a long wait!

Wife, I'm asking you to act in a way that demonstrates that the person God has placed in the middle of your life story is someone with great value.

Jesus talked about this when he said, "Where your treasure is, there your heart will be also" (Matthew 6:21, ESV). In short, when you start valuing something or someone, your feelings for that thing or person will begin to change as well!

The second picture of *blessing* carries the idea of weight or value—like adding coins to an ancient scale. The greater the weight, the higher the value. If our attitude is that our spouse has high value, then our actions towards them are reflected in the second picture: adding "weighty" words and actions to show value.

Think about how we bless the Lord. When we say that (or sing those words), we're really saying, "Lord, you're so valuable, I bow the knee before you." But then we add our praise to him. In short, when we bless someone, we acknowledge in our heart that that person has great worth and value, and then we act on that by adding to their life through blessings!

Because our spouse is so valuable, our blessing of them adds to their life, like adding a coin to a scale. It's means we make the decision to add more value to them: "Since God has given you to me as my husband, my completer, helper, lover, companion, and friend, I'm choosing to add to your life."

And as C. S. Lewis said, when you choose to do some of these small, positive things, you'll see good "increase at compound interest" and you'll bless your marriage, your family, and your future!

Blessing is a hugely better choice than its opposite: to curse. (Remember, we're to choose blessing over curse.). In Scripture, the word *curse* suggests doom or at the very least misery; it's as if life-giving water is taken away from someone. That's a terrible picture. I'm not going to spend time focusing on how we subtract from others. That just comes naturally from our fallen nature and our poor choices. We can choose to subtract our love and encouragement. And let me emphasize that it *is* a choice, not something anyone made us do.

My prayer for you is that you will choose life over death, blessing over curse. And I pray that you'll live out that choice starting today.

Starting a Revolution

Reading this book and putting its ideas to use (and perhaps getting another copy and sharing it with a friend or relative who will hold you accountable to be a woman of blessing for your husband) can be nothing short of *revolutionary*. That means that blessing your husband can bring about a fundamental or major change in the relationship you have with your husband and the culture you establish in your home.

It's *revolutionary* to come to Christ and to see him turn us into a new creature (2 Corinthians 5:17). It's *revolutionary* that Jesus gave up his life so that we could have eternal life (John 3:16). That same kind of revolutionary, crazy, transformational love that Jesus pours out on you who know him is nothing short of the kind of love that you're to have for your spouse! Jesus "has blessed you in the heavenly realms with every spiritual blessing in Christ" (Ephesians 1:3, NIV), and you can enjoy all of those blessings now. And you're called on to love your husband—to build into his life—to choose to bless him as well!

LET THE
BLESSING BEGIN

WIFE, YOU HAVE a sphere of influence with your husband that no one else has. I pray that you are encouraged to use that influence to bless your husband like no one else can. Through meaningful touch, spoken words of high value, picturing a special future, and an active commitment to your husband, you can pass on the incredible gift of the blessing. I hope that you have found some helpful ideas in this book as you embark on a journey to bless your husband and to bless others. I'm praying for you on your journey:

Lord, may you bless
this woman who holds this book. Thank you
that she's read it and that she's committed
now to start to bless her husband. Lord, he
is a gift from you.

No matter the challenges or trials
this couple has been through or may
encounter, Lord, may this woman know the
truth of how actions dictate feelings,
not the other way around.
Her decision and choice to bless her
husband is something you will honor.

Finally, Lord, help this wife to know that
small things can begin to change everything.
You, Jesus, talked about that
when you shared that faith the size of a tiny
mustard seed can move a mountain
[Matthew 17:20]. Lord, may these small
things (and other similar things this wife
comes up with) bring great things to her
marriage as she gives and lives the blessing.

> *Now, Lord, may these small ideas and thoughts be like that God-blessed mustard seed that, based on your love and blessing, blooms into a new season of love and life for this couple. And may every new season of life for this couple be one filled with your light, love, life, and blessing.*

Notes

1. This section adapted from John Trent and Gary Smalley, *The Blessing*, (Nashville: Thomas Nelson, 2011)

2. Word picture examples taken from *The Language of Love* by Gary Smalley and John Trent, a Focus on the Family book published by Tyndale House Publishers, Inc. © 1988, 1991, 2006 Gary Smalley and John Trent. Used by permission.

Bring the Blessing to Your Home

A spouse's or a parent's approval affects the way people view themselves. You can give your spouse and/or your children the gift of unconditional acceptance the Bible calls the blessing. This set of four short booklets is packed with tips on what the blessing is, and each booklet gives 30 ideas on how to give it to those around you. Even if you didn't get the blessing as a child, you can learn to give it to others.

Author John Trent is a Christian psychologist and co-author of the million-copy bestselling book, *The Blessing*. He shares his own story of his father's abandonment, and how he learned to give the blessing to his children.

Paperback, 112 pages, 4.5 x 6.5 x .25 inches

30 Ways a Father Can Bless His Children
9781628622775   4077X

30 Ways a Mother Can Bless Her Children
9781628622805   4078X

30 Ways a Husband Can Bless His Wife
9781628622836   4079X

30 Ways a Wife Can Bless Her Husband
9781628622867   4080X

Get 10 more tips!
FREE! Download 10 More Ways to be a Blessing
to Those Around You.
Go to — BlessingChallenge.com